The Human Condition
The Poet's Perspective

By

Brian Sankarsingh

Including poems by
J. L. Kaytor
J. E. Rehel
Loretta Laurie Fisher
Sherman K. Francis and

And featuring poems by
Jayson~Tyler Sankarsingh and
Lincoln Alexander Estridge

BRIAN SANKARSINGH POETRY

Brian Sankarsingh Books
581 Millard St
Stouffville, ON L4A 7Y4
Canada

www.brianthepoet.com

ISBN
978-1-7777968-1-5 (eBook)
978-1-7777968-0-8 (Paperback)

1.   Poetry, Canadian

Dedications

This book is dedicated to my life partner Jay who, by example, taught me patience, tolerance, and serenity. She is my lighthouse in the dark night, my shelter in the raging storm, my succor in times of trouble and the bedrock of my love – **Brian Sankarsingh**

This is dedicated to Tony and Nick who have gotten me through so many highs and lows. Your love and support throughout this new adventure in my life means everything to me, and I couldn't do it without you both. To Rob, who was my heart, and to Jeff, I love you all so much – **J. L. Kaytor**

To E.S., B.R., M.W. — and all grandmothers. Thank you for your patience, your wisdom and your love to help us through difficult times. To the co-authors, for your tenacity and generosity of spirit and mind – **J. E. Rehel**

This is dedicated to my African Ancestors, to my daughters and my grandson, to my W.A.C. and SpringMag comrades, and to my Anthology team headed by Brian Sankarsingh – **Loretta Laurie Fisher**

I would like to dedicate my work to my dear friend and mother Karen Nurse who inspired me to write poetry and to my ever supporting and ever-loving wife Lisa. I would also like to dedicate these poems to my children Isaiah, Jovan, Jazara and Jedediah, may they also be inspired to write – **Sherman K. Francis**

This is dedicated to my family as well as the friends who have helped shape and inspire my work - **Jayson-Tyler Sankarsingh**

This is dedicated to those whose lives were taken due to police brutality; as individuals who didn't choose to die but rather their lives were stolen from them. This is dedicated to my mom for instilling knowledge in me to analyze the world with a critical race lens. Dedicated to my girlfriend Danielle Des Vignes for helping me critically assess my empathy daily. Lastly, to Prof. María J. Méndez for prompting me to investigate the legacy of colonialism and how it affects my personal life - **Lincoln Alexander Estridge**

Acknowledgement

The Human Condition is my second book in as many years. Indeed, writers and poets have had lots of time, opportunity and material to draw on since the pandemic and lockdowns began in early 2020. Although not intentional, this book is a continuation of my first book as it continues to dive into social and emotional challenges, we've all faced. There is, however, a significant addition to this work. It now includes the poems of several emerging and established poets. These talented people came into my life, at times, unannounced and unexpected but I am supremely grateful for them all.

The Human Condition, The Poet's Perspective is divided into three parts. First, it delves into some of the many challenges that humanity faced during the interminably long COVID-19 lockdown. Then in the title section, it takes you on a journey of the human condition; peeking into the cracks and crevasses that make us who we are and exploring the highs and lows we all face. Finally, in Let's Talk Racism it shines a light on the evils of racism.

Creativity presents itself in various forms such
as music, dance, art, and literature. Belittle,
ignore, and cast them aside at your peril for they
hold the essential nourishment we all need to
realize our full human potential. They can
inspire us in our struggle; ease the burden of our
heartache; galvanize us into action; soothe the
beast within us and plant the seeds of hope in
the driest desert. I hope, dear reader that here
you find some little reflection of yourself and as
you turn the pages you leave some of your own
uniqueness between the lines.

Table of Contents

Reflecting on COVID-19

Saving Our Humanity

Silently, the monster moves, from one victim to another
Hungrily seeking to infect your child, your wife, your mother
It does not care who you are whether President or pauper
Coronavirus is on the prowl taking lives and raiding coffers

This virus serves to remind us of our innate humanity
Illustrating our fragility and exposing our mortality
There lies a fear that can reveal the worst of our behaviour
Ignoring all else but ourselves forgetting friends and neighbours

Hoarding toilet paper exposes the depravity of our minds
Not thinking of each other, just our own behinds
When will we ever realize that for humans to survive?
We must care for each other not just the people in our lives

Would that we had leaders who could think outside the box

Those who seek solutions not just putting up
roadblocks
If we hope to survive, by hoarding face masks
and supplies
That's a stain on our humanity, we can never
sanitize

Caring for those at most risk, should be our
main concern
Let's choose to be magnanimous, not selfish or
taciturn
If history has taught us anything, it's that when
we act together
Collaboration changes us and makes us all the
better

As you stay at home today, think deeply about
this time
Nothing else is important in this current
paradigm
Coronavirus is on the prowl, some won't make it
out alive
But if we stick together, our humanity might
survive

A COVID Conversation

Conspiracy we cry
They're trying to control our lives
Forcing us against our will
Making mountains of molehills
Stay six feet apart we're told
This is not just any cold
Don't go out, don't congregate
Or you'll make it circulate

If you go out, you have one task
Remember you must wear a mask
We do this to stop the disease
And even then, there are no guarantees

Hey, you can't tell me what to do
To myself, I must be true
You're trying to control my life
This will lead to war and strife
You're crippling our economy
With lies and fake biology
Don't stop me from being free
I'm not a guinea pig from Tuskegee

Are you kidding? We're saving lives
What's this talk about backstabbing knives?
Thousands have died, and more will too
Listen to what we're saying to you
This isn't some shady experiment

In fact, we have the evidence
It's not just here, this is worldwide
Many people have not survived
If we knew and didn't act
You'd say that we were hiding facts
You'd say we were culling the herd
In your theatre of the absurd
In your eyes, there is no right
Try as we will, try as we might
Conspiracies buried everywhere
Conspiracies made to ensnare
Often the opposite is true
And the thing you misconstrue
To be a big conspiracy
Is your enthusiastic apathy

They Need Not Die Alone

By Sherman K. Francis

Conception required contributing parts
A love that flowed from two beating hearts
From the day their eyes were miraculously open
The chain of companionship would be woven
The love they shared with ones so dear,
At their final breath should it not be there?

Someone was there when the first tooth was lost
There to watch the ball they first tossed
Some were there as foolish acts were dared
Others gathered as accomplishments shared
Now they lay contemplating their last,
No one to comfort as from this life they passed?

Who deliberated such a decision?
One surely made without compassion
For a hand to hold is without exception
Far better than any medical concoction
Left to lie in total solitude,
Is this all that their lives have accrued?

It should be looked upon as utter cruelty
Proposing protection with no civility
For man to live alone was a thing God didn't
uphold

Nor should he die without a familiar hand to
hold
The turmoil and pain in a spirit that knows its
departing
Wouldn't they welcome comforting words from
love one's imparting? □
Locked in life's house that will soon be
destroyed
Destiny controlled by those rendered paranoid
If only they knew that this would be their end
That mortal visit would be one to contend
This mysterious virus and the restriction we
condone
Shouldn't common sense tell you they need not
die alone?

Social Distancing goes awry

Darkness descends into the blackness of my
personal despair
Trapped in the recesses of my calloused mind
Don't worry pretty darling, Misery is here
Let us embrace each other during quarantine
There is no point in fighting it, no reason to deny
We desire the cocoon not the butterfly
Avoiding other people is what we prefer to do
Braced in against the outside and never to
breakthrough
Please my darling let's not dwell on what might
be
Misery may love company, but we want solitude
Away from mindless banter and pointless
repartee

Your Money or Your Life

Money or Lives, what would you choose?
This is the debate that's now making the news
Our economy is suffering, businesses on the
edge
Politicians declare there are no more bets to
hedge
Medical experts say, making people go back too
fast
Means the present count of victims, will be
needlessly surpassed

Economy or Family, what would your option be
Would you risk a loved one's life, to protect
financial security?
Those at risk of dying have an underlying
condition
This may be a mercy, not a drastic course
correction
Are you willing to give your life, so the economy
recovers?
Billions of dollars will be saved but is it just
about the numbers?

What message are we sending, when we choose
one or the other
Can we measure the worth of sisters, mothers,
fathers, brothers?

Are we sacrificing people's lives for the almighty
dollar?
Or are we willing to do whatever it takes, for
them to recover
History will judge us all, whatever course we
choose
Future generations will decide, to congratulate
or accuse

It's not just black and white, there are many
shades at play
What we now believe, might not be true at the
end of the day
We're subjected to biased reporting from the
press
It doesn't matter if they're the Right or Left
How can we discern what's truth from fiction?
When we choose to believe based on ideological
predilection

SOS COVID

By Sherman K. Francis

Hey you! The constant complainer
Everything must go your way and
What's coming, must come sooner
Griping about mask and shield for your eye
Pause for a moment and think
Of those who have died
You have life, a gift worth cherishing
So, give a little thought for those perishing

Hey you! Freedom's champion
To be free is a right but loving and
Caring is far greater, but that's my opinion
The precautions you're being asked to take
Could save you from that grave mistake
Disagree? Still go along with the principle
So, onlookers could see you've set the right
example

Hey you! Bereaved and confused
It's not everything you hear is truth
So, stop imbibing every piece of news
That burro could bray and do a lot with twitter
For him lying is exercise that makes him
stronger
If you want facts, he is certainly not the source

He only leads the innocent to take the wrong course

Hey you! The brave and courageous
Analyze and trust the facts
This virus is really contagious
Protecting yourself should be your main focus
Stand strong, stand firm and never waver
And if attacked, give it your best fight
Though in this gloomy tunnel, you shall see the light

Perfidious

Special thanks to Jennifer Sukhu for suggesting the
name of this poem

We see connections even when you think they
don't exist
Every word and every action combined with a
subtle twist
We can pierce their veil of lies our minds are in
sharp focus
Teasing nuances from their speech smoking out
the bogus

We have the right to protest, so that is what we'll
do
It doesn't really matter if our actions spread the
'China flu'
You cannot tell us what to do, force us to stay
inside
Our freedoms bought and paid for, it will be
glorified

We don't trust the government or anyone with
power
They just want to rule us all, as they sit in ivory
towers
We will not be sheeple , blindly led out to be
slaughtered

We refuse to be an offering, to be burnt upon
their altar

It doesn't matter what they say or do, we know
the games they play
We operate in black or white, while they use
shades of grey
Ignore their drivel, listen to us, and discern the
truth from lies
Or you'll remain in servitude to their evil
enterprise

Even mundane ideas, with words, can be made
great
Words indeed have the power, to unite or
separate
There's no monopoly on truth, no one owns it all
And any man who says he does is being
hypocritical!

Reflecting on COVID-19

By J. L. Kaytor

Come and sit beside me she said
I'll lend a gentle ear
Tell me all your worries
Your words are for me to hear

I offer you solace and kindness
My arms are open wide
Come to me if you are in need
For I too have also cried

This time has been hard for everyone
No one knew what to do
We are still feeling the confusion
Of dealing with something so new

Will anyone ever fully understand
About how this has changed us all
Will we ever make sense of everything?
When our memories do recall

Will our planet ever change?
Will we ever completely heal
Or is this our new reality
For something that is so real

The Unknown Virus

By Sherman K. Francis

Protect yourselves its coming hard
This virus they're proclaiming
More deadly than the flu, or not that bad
The experts try explaining
Oh what is it, oh what is it that pains the world
so?
In a nutshell we can say, they simply do not
know
Wear a mask, don't wear a mask
The masses in sheer confusion
Twill curb the spread really fast
Or another fool's illusion
This deadly thing, once contracted is it to the
grave you go?
The answer here is not so clear, they simply do
not know

Politics now play a part
For an important health decision
Choices made from the start
Depends on one's affiliation
Who to trust, science or the status quo?
To you again I must submit, they simply do not
know

Men are dying left and right
With this invisible enemy
Shut everything down, shut it tight
Orders barked at you and me
When will we ever learn to stop moving with the
flow?
Those in charge will never admit, they simply do
not know

Social distancing to board a plane
Cheap flights, prices you cannot beat
Then stuffed to the back like sardines
Crammed tightly with knees touching the seat
Bail out money in hand as the nation's debt
continues to grow
Did the virus cause it? They simply don't know

Staying home, this time was a plus
To work no one wants to go back
All credit due to the great stimulus
And that's the simple fact
Much more than my salary and the economy
slow?
Ask the puppet leaders, they simply don't know

Whether Chinese, Italian or French
This virus wreaking havoc all over the world
Yet leaders only concern is putting judges on the
bench
Without care for the rising death toll

How you get it the evidence doesn't clearly
show
Everyone's an expert and they simply don't
know

Agree to Disagree

NOTE FROM THE POET - The challenge of this
poem was twofold. One was to use consecutive lines
in the earlier stanza. So, stanza two starts with the
second line of stanza one, stanza three starts with the
third line from stanza two and stanza four starts with
the fourth like of stanza three. The next challenge
was to end stanza four with the opening line of
stanza one

Should I still call you friend if your view differs
from mine
This thinking doesn't unify it only misaligns
Iron sharpens iron we must have space for
debate
If we can't disagree without enmity, it may
already be too late

This thinking doesn't unify, it only misaligns
No one man holds all the truth or else he'd be
divine
God doesn't speak to only one man His word is
for all to hear
Any man who says he speaks for God aspires to
be a puppeteer

God doesn't speak to only one man His word is
for all to hear
You don't hold the keys to heaven, you are no
saviour

Instead let's agree to disagree, and vigorously so
Let's contest every idea and question the status
quo

Let's contest every idea and question the status
quo
This is how we progress; how humanity grows
So, if I believe in science and you in the divine
Should I still call you friend if your view differs
from mine

Alone

By J. L. Kaytor

In March 2020
When the world went to hell
He remained alone closed off from the world
For many months he stayed hidden
Fearful … afraid … anxious
After 3 months of frustration
He gathered all his courage
And went outside among people

He was immediately intimidated by his
surroundings
He felt a panic attack coming that he could not
avoid
He wanted to run and hide, to go back to his safe
place
With no people
To be alone
Walking quickly back to the car
He went home

Over a year later he can go outside
And be among people, at a distance
But only for a very, very short time
Or the anxiety and the panic come back
He wants to feel free
He wants to be happy

He wants life to be 'normal'
But what is feeling free
Or being happy
Or above all else - what is normal
Will he ever have the freedom he felt before all
of this started
What is life without feeling discouraged
Despondent
Worried

What happens when there are
No masks
No hand sanitizers
No fear of someone coughing or sneezing
Will this really change how he feels
Is it possible to feel no fear, no sadness?
To feel safe, to feel happy, everywhere
To feel good about life and about the world
To not worry about the uncertainty of anything

He is told to talk to someone about his feelings
But that fills him with apprehension
What if someone tells him he's not normal
What if someone tells him to just 'suck it up'
Right now, he can't do it
The depression, the fear is real

SO REAL

So still, he hides
Where no one can see him

Because it's safe there
Alone

The Human Condition

The Abuser

She deserves it
She had it coming
She doesn't listen
I gave her warning
Now she's crying
It's driving me crazy
I work so hard
And she's so lazy

Another slap
Just stop your whining
I need some quiet
Stop you're moaning
I fall asleep
Drunk out of my gourd
She finally shut up
The stupid broad

Sure, I love her
But she often needs
A harsh reminder
Of her misdeeds
Awake next morning
With a pounding head
Knuckles sore
And cherry red
I call her name

And hurriedly
She says "I'm coming"
Worriedly □
Her face is bruised
Purple and black
Did I do that?
Another attack?

I'm sorry baby
What have I done?
Didn't mean to hurt you
You know you're the one
She smiles and whispers
I love you too
I know how hard
It's been for you

She makes me breakfast
Everything's alright
Until I get drunk
Again tonight

The Abused

I loved that man with all my heart
This heart that beats no more
I was so sure, right from the start
Our love would make us stand apart, together
forevermore

His love for me was very strong
Though it often caused me pain
Don't judge me now, you'd be so wrong
He's not so bad, just headstrong, I don't need to
explain

He only hits me when I'm at fault
When I forget what he asks me for
Keep in mind, we're both adults
Please do not use the word assault that only
angers him even more

That other time, he was just stressed
His boss insulted him that day
When he came home, he was a mess
With his anger so repressed, don't you dare to
inveigh!

Last night the neighbours called the cops
I guess they heard me cry
It was my fault, he could not stop

Nosy neighbours just eavesdrop, that must be the reason why

"I love you baby, you're the one!"
He shouts as they take him away
Something inside me becomes undone
A fear that I cannot outrun, and it causes me dismay☐
Several months have now gone by
I'm free from pain and dread
No purple bruise and no black eye
No beating if I don't comply, my life seems rosy red

Then he showed up at my work
My fears, once gone, are back
Screaming my name, he was berserk
Face contorted with a smirk, I prepare for his attack

Lying here in pain and crying
From the start, this was his plan
Life no longer terrifying
His words echo as I lay dying, "If I can't have you, no one can!"

Reflection(s) on Loss

By J. E Rehel

Mirrors favoured us for a bit—
In the beginning,
Of our
Crisis.

We saw ourselves in each other—

Empathy abounded, for a time—

Giving way to the moments between where it
began to happen
To us,
And when it fully enveloped to become us,
Evaporated like the tea I spilled, two days ago
And haven't had the heart yet to
Wipe up.

"Stop searching," says my 18-month pandemic
self to my 9-month pandemic self. "Give it a rest,
and your spirit. Go and be with yourself first, so
deeply that you'd never, ever
Fall out of love
With you.
And Life.

All of it—every last bulb of new growth and
celebration of ends, and all that fertile ground
between—carry it carefully with your
Reverence, embodied in the everyday, in your
breaths, expressions, exchanges and words left
hanging alone in thought, not yet lost (entirely)
beneath our thousands and millions of masks
Real and hidden.☐
"Leave yourself always enchanted," they
whisper to themselves, unchained and granted,
At last, a small shred of wisdom unlocked, from
months spent and imagined lost,
Unhooked, unmoored and cast off, not from
others but with and from
one's lonesome self.

Still, the gap between self-
Awareness and self-distortion appears, and then
Seems to disappear and deftly
make its way to the heart of the matter,
To the heart
Of us,
Through all of this. The breaths and beaming
and sighs beyond of grief
And re-seaming, give way to our fossilized
memories, pulled from the reef
Of history by time's unrelenting tides and brief
shards of shared mystery.

Hope

By Jayson~Tyler Sankarsingh

They say that the eye is the passage
To the truth that lies within
Yet entry has proven a challenge
Much to my chagrin

As time takes its toll on my body
And experience adds to my wisdom
I find myself perched rather oddly
Between hope and cynicism

On one hand, the pain that has haunted me
Beckons my heart to close its doors
As its evidence it uses society
And all its anger, hatred, and wars

But alas, she whispers to me sweetly
"With our own evils must we cope
And, though good, no one said it was easy
To live life holding on to hope"

And in the face of this beauty
I am robbed of the will to oppose
And hence I take it as my duty
To view life through lenses colored rose.

The Great Dichotomy

We all want to succeed in the dreams we pursue
Motivated with passion and drive
We fight to achieve and make those dreams
come true
It's the passion that keeps us alive

Reach for the stars we are taught to pursue
If you fail, to the treetops you'll fall
Spend your life searching for a breakthrough
But keep your eyes on the ball

What we don't learn when we overachieve
Is surviving when dreams don't come true
Caught up in the chase we refuse to believe
That our hopes and our plans could ever fall
through

Now we face a great dichotomy
A mark of the human condition
Success is more than fame or celebrity
More than triumph by a process of attrition

Success is the belief we have in ourselves
Being comfortable in one's own skin
Success isn't learned on musty bookshelves
It's not only learned if we win

It's permitting ourselves to fail
But adamantly never giving in
Planning and working to ensure we prevail
Should be our mindset before we begin

No One is Illegal

By Loretta Laurie Fisher

No human is illegal, we must stress this again
and again
But immigration authorities' act like it's just a
casual game
They are free to follow us, tag us and say:
"You're It!"
Plucking us right out of our lives into a
bottomless pit
Detention centres are well-funded & aren't
broken one bit
They work fine as originally designed: a
heartbreaking trick
built especially for those dreaming of a nice
place to embark
But Brown and Black families are set-up to be
torn apart
Hunted down by N. American eagles with eyes
too sharp!
Head-hunters with hearts cold like ICE throw us
into the dark dungeons called immigration
detention centres
It's a slap in the face and a living nightmare!
The 'so-called real canadians' live their lives
unaware:
privileged citizens with a free pass to walk by
uninterrupted

The immigration system hasn't failed to prove
it's corrupted!
Those of African descent feeling defeated,
routinely cheated
Of our rights to travel freely and to live life
unimpeded
The dark skin we're in makes part of my kin into
unfair game: 'maybe you can stay; maybe we'll
send you back home again'
Black & Brown people are deliberately forgotten
and detained
Unless it's declared we are needed to pick
farmers' crops
or fill the most laborious tasks, all the lowest
paying jobs
When high education's achieved it's disregarded
and excluded
Our labour in detention centres & prisons is still
being looted
by colonial minded magnates capitalizing on us
for their financial use
Magnates grow obscenely rich from this
continued abuse!
Unwitting migrant workers line up to board this
crazy caboose
Human beings of this planet: Together we must
break loose!
Believe me. If we are not all free, then none of us
will be!

The Gardener

By Jayson~Tyler Sankarsingh

The crack of dawn sees his eyes open
And a new day of labour begins
He turns, again, to his devotion
As his face is lit up by his grin

Some see his work as a pastime
While others would call it a chore
But he smiles through dirt as well as grime
For this, anything he'd endure

Some ask him, 'Why do you do this
When there's so much more you can achieve?'
He replies, 'In their presence I find bliss
Their beauty is all that I need.'

So each day since, he wakes to his flowers
A frown on his face one shan't find
And he tends to them, daily, for hours
They are paramount in his mind.

Us (I found you/You found me)

By J. E. Rehel

I found a baby bird,
Fallen from a branch high above our heads,
On the hardened spring snow
Of the forest floor.

Alive with fragile life, and healthy,
But not borne by time's tides to the right
address.

We scooped it up together, weaving
our
hands
to form a nest.
The fragile life tied us to each other for a
moment,
on these frozen lands.

Brazen spring sunlight glared at us
Through empty branches. No
Mothers in sight save who could have been,
what might still be.

Spring's warmth weeks off,
the nest already empty,
we walked on. Life had come and gone from our
grasp, where we nested briefly.

Now unbraided, we saw our ends, uprooted,
fated;
And given to each other and the forest, we found
fragile life again in each other's best spirits. You
made us tea
on a small flame, and offered me some biscuits.

Later on we parked our cars close,
Loosened our masks, and gazed into each
other's hopeful faces in the darkening plaza
parking spaces.
You reached your arms out the passenger
window, like vines stretching across the gulf
between us. I met the grasp of your hands
hungrily, still at arm's length, but connected at
last, in the pale neon twilight.

We found each other on
the frozen forest floor,
on the hard pavement,
hearts stretched and faded,
and then drove off separately, alone in dusk's
shadows with our weary, and oft-broken hearts
lamented, sated,
if just for a moment.

The Cactus

By Jayson~Tyler Sankarsingh

She sat in her yellow pot,
In her dry, dusty soil
That she loved.

And the green of her skin
Brought out the white of her flowers.
And her spines
Were small and blunt.
And she was blooming.

And within her was her water
That she offered
To any passing by.

So he came,
Because he was thirsty.
But her water was never sweet enough,
Never crisp enough.
So he tried to make her better.

He sat her in a gray pot,
Filled with moist, earthy soil
That choked her roots.

And her skin became brown,
And her white flowers fell.

And her spines
Grew vast and sharp.
And she was withering.

And still she held her water,
And still she let him drink;
Though her flavor never changed.

So he left,
Because he was frustrated.
Still she was not sweet enough,
Not crisp enough.
So he had to find one better.

Impostor Syndrome

I struggle with what I am
With so-called success and accolades
Playing society's useless charades
While trapped in my mental stockade
A literary jack-of-all-trades

I grapple with what they say I am
My talent seems mediocre
I grapple with the moniker
A wordsmith or chronicler
Or poetic compositor

I am unsure what I am
A word slinging poetic pretender
Never the champion, always a contender
A nauseating literary offender
Who despite the odds doesn't want to
surrender?

There is a name for this
Impostor syndrome
It's shiny but doesn't believe it's chrome
So that when it's left alone
It goes back to feeling it doesn't belong

I am sure of the path I must take
To myself, I must be true
Be it a good or bad review

Challenges I must pass through
To finally share these words with you
□
Listen to me well my friend
Through your doubt and anxiety
Fleeing from your insanity
You must believe in your ability
To share your message with humanity

The Seat

I make my nightly trip
Eyes half-closed and sleepy
I'm careful not to slip
But I really need to pee-pee

Feeling around in the dark
Looking forward to relief so sweet
 I let out a screaming bark
The man didn't put down the seat

The Social Media Warrior

Sitting behind my keyboard
The monitor lighting my face
I take on a different personality
One with much less grace
I become a fearless warrior
Insults become my mace
I will tell you like it is
No preamble or preface
Shut up, sit down I'm speaking
You better learn your place
The knowledge of the world is mine
A lord of time and space
I don't care if you're an immigrant
You can go back to your birthplace
I don't care if you're gay or lesbian
That's not a lifestyle I embrace
I don't care if you are black or brown
So please don't bring up race
I just need to voice my opinion
I need to state my case
So, if you're weak or fragile
Better do an about-face
This conversation's not for you
I'm about to pick up the pace
You come here to my country
To democracy's showcase
You try to change my history
But I will not let you erase

My glorious ancestors past
You will never replace
I am a social media warrior
In the Social Media arms race
If I have something to say I'll say it
But probably not to your face

Social Media

Craving 'likes' is just my addiction
Measuring my happiness through your attention
The more I have, the more I want
I am a Social Media dilettante

Hoping that my next post goes viral
I'll do anything, even at my peril
Trending upward is my only desire
To be the one that you respect and admire

I don't have anything meaningful to share
But I want the world to know that I am here
Increase my followers, increase my views
Mindlessly chasing the Social Media Muse

Agony

It bites into my body
Ripping gashes as it flows
Each wave makes my mind cloudy
As it amplifies and grows
Wave after wave washes over me
Into much deeper water
God, I pray, please set me free
As I shake and as I shudder.
Lightning bolts of searing pain
Clarity in each ebb and flow
I scream out to Mary Jane
In a shaky staccato
How much more can one man bear
Filled with agony and doubt
Before he cries out in despair
And finally passes out

The Survivor

Devilishly funny,
His witty comebacks
Draw us into his comical web
The wrinkles on this time-worn face
Tells stories of a life
Well lived
Well accustomed to laughter

A heart, open to possibilities
Willing to be captured
His once shrewd mind
Slightly dulled by a memory stealing syndrome
Still manages, to conceive
razor-sharp comebacks and friendly banter
He makes me wonder about
the storehouse of memories
he could spend countless hours recounting

A veteran of wars
and life
of pain
and strife
A warrior who took all
that life could throw at him
and gave back his weight in gold
 How I wonder
should I end this poem?
Can any poet ever really capture?

the fullness of such a life?
For ending on a good note seems banal
yet ending on a bad one too cliché

Endings are so overrated anyway

The Siamese Twins

The Siamese twins are at it again
They're War and Civilization
Alone or together, they despise each other
Bitter enemies and loving brothers

One relentlessly seeking souls
The other strives for less morbid goals
Peacefully they cannot exist
Pull them apart, they will resist

Fuelled by emotive rage
War cannot be assuaged
Falsely promising his sibling
Soon there'll be no more need for killing

Just this one tribe left to subdue
They must not win we must follow through
Civilization hesitatingly agrees
With a rueful smile, War applies the squeeze

Civilization sits on the defence
Protecting one's own is no offence
He can't stop thinking of 'the other'
Weren't they too, sons, fathers, brothers?

Must we fight? What are we trying to save?
Aren't we just feeding fodder to the grave?
But sinking a knife of peace into War's bosom

Wouldn't that be an ironic schism?

Killing always leads to just more killing
Peace through bloodshed slaughters the
unwilling
Unless we stop trading in people's lives
We will never, ever sheath our knives

Yet Civilization turns a blind eye
And supports his brother's alibi
The lie that Civilization cannot exist
Without the clenching of War's fist

Big Blue

Tick-tock, tick-tock.
I count the seconds as they sing
Is that Big Blue calling out to me
"Hey you! I'm buh-lue for y-ewe!"
Hours meld into each other
What?
Who?
Blue is that you?
Reality's metamorphosis continues
The mist continues to thicken
An eerie sound of solitude
Punctured only by the
Tick -tock of the clock

Some trees at the end of the
Driveway pick up their roots and move on
So, what am I still waiting for?
Tick tock goes the clock
I reach out, only to find an empty nest
Or is it emptiness?
My humanity teeters on the brink
I'll hunker down to wait it out
Intent to survive
Determined to outlive
The apocalypse

While others merrily dance
In the dark wet streets

Sticking out their middle fingers.
"Come get me, I don't care!
My purpose is to dance and so I shall!"
The endless parade of souls
Continue on their dusty way
Tick-tock goes the clock!
I ask Blue "What shall we remember?
What have we learned?
Will we be better or worse for the experience?"
Blue?
Are you still there?

Sacrifice

Can sacrifice
Bring balance to
The chaos
of life?

What's so important
And time-consuming that I
can not
will not
give it up to make
another's life better?

Even if,
That other is me?

Do Unto Others

Why do we judge others?
But deny that we do no wrong
Why is it that we'd rather
Think the worst of our fellowman
We expect bad things from a stranger
But are hurt when others do the same
Using the excuse of danger
In this terribly selfish game
What happened to the golden rule?
It's been turned inside out
Now everyone else is a fool
But you know what everyone's about
So, you lock yourself in a cocoon
"Why do I need to do you a favour"
You think that makes you immune
When in fact it's the lowest behaviour
It may seem like I'm a ridiculous person
A sucker, an SJW , a fool
But there are many other things worse than
Choosing to believe that not everyone's cruel.

Discernment

Darkness isn't always evil's companion
As many of us might believe
The light can often host Mammon
Morality with malice up its sleeve

Never judge books by their cover
For covers can often belie
The story you may discover
Will condemn before it will deify

Let all by their words and actions be judged
No favour or fondness abide
Decency will never begrudge
Where true morality chooses to reside

A shared enemy doesn't make you a friend
Hatred is not just black or white
Friendship on one's actions depends
Opposition does not always unite

Be careful in whom you choose to confide
Not everyone can be called friend
All snakes may not choose dens to hide
Discernment will always win in the end

Opulence

I can't draw pictures
I don't do art
I've got no voice
To sing that part

I can't build buildings
Can barely dance
Don't believe me?
Then take your chance

Don't have big muscles
Can barely run
I walk upstairs
And that's it, I'm done

Can't drive buses
Can't drive a truck
Can't cut your hair
And that's your luck

Deliver mail?
In snow, sleet or rain?
Not me buddy
So, think again

Can't serve you coffee
Hot chocolate or tea
You'd be wearing it and
That'd be it for me

Can't work with numbers
Nope, can't cut your grass
Can't wait on tables
That'll be a hard pass

Can't fix computers
Or shovel snow
Can't work at heights
Oh no, no, no!!
 Can't take your orders
Or hammer a nail
If I do your taxes
You'd be in jail

Can't be a lawyer
Can't be a judge
Can't clean your sewers
'Cos, I hate sludge

Can't drive a taxi
Or sweep the street
Can't build a robot
Though that'd be neat

Don't have the talent
But guess what honey
Don't need to bother
'Cos, I got money

Nestled in

This poem was inspired by a piece of the same name
by talented painter Ray McNeice

A house isn't always where the heart is
Nor often where it longs to be
It's not always a place of peace
Or a sanctuary of safety
A long and lonely driveway
Guarded by a magnificent tree
Leading to a front door
There's not much left to see
But this house is like no other
Love overflows to the street
A place of joy and refuge
A place for hearts to meet
Gazing past its leafy sentinel
To the home set deep within
It's not so much hidden
As it's safely nestled in

Poets

Poets are the conscience
of our humanity
They challenge us to dream
of things we cannot yet see
They dare us to look at life
from a different perspective
Poets are the last vestiges
of love's eternal rhythms
They create music in chaos
and manifest beauty in death
Poets are the fools
in Society's inner court
They treat the law as an ass
raising challenge to our every thought
They question every judgement
and judge every decision

Woe to a world without poets
A bleak world
A sad world
A world destitute of love
A place of ashes and sorrow

The Letter

His smell lingers in the musty bedroom air
His side of the bed still unslept
A thought begins to gnaw, a doubt, a fear
One she was still unwilling to accept

He'd been spending more time away from her
Work consumed all his time
Now she felt all alone without succour
Marriage without reason, love without rhyme.

One thirty a.m. the door quietly closes
Fear grips her heart like a vice
Doubt like a wild monstrosity grows
Would her heart pay the final price?

She hears him moving around in the kitchen
A beer bottle cap falls to the floor
She held her breath to better listen
And the doubt keeps on eating her core

It went quiet for an hour or more
Did he fall asleep on the chair?
Not a sound, not a breath or a snore
Now the doubt consumed even the air

Quietly she went down the stairs
Maybe she would just bring him to bed
In this moment she realizes her fears
Through a letter on the counter unread

The Mastery of Lies

Special thanks to Roberta Shaffer-Singh for
suggesting the name of this poem

Lies are like mazes with twists and with turns
Filled with pits and mysterious caverns.
Labyrinthine innuendos to baffle the mind
Lies that confuse and lies that spellbind

Falsehoods like serpents with venomous fangs
Not just in tweets but in lengthy harangues.
Flickering tongue tasting the fruit of its toil
Lies everywhere as the serpent uncoils

Who can we trust to tell us what's true?
Can we ever find honesty in this deceitful
milieu?
Is truth even a thing that we need anymore?
Is this the age of the provocateur?

If everything is false unless I believe
There is no truth to test the lies that we weave
What kind of impact does this have on our
future?
Will this not tear our society asunder?

Words aren't just words and I hope you agree
They are still now as they were anciently
Words can overthrow despicable tyrants

Words are the things that give power to peasants

Truth must be tested through discourse and
debate,
No single person can ever dictate
For the truth by its nature is owned by all
people,
This is how we defeat everything that's deceitful □

Solidarity

By Loretta Laurie Fisher

So many of us still in invisible service; but a few
used as tokens in a hostile hierarchy.
So many in precarious jobs with no benefits &
not enough pay to help our families escape
poverty!
Contracted to the lowest bidder for menial jobs
indefinitely
Think about who they invited to always work in
a factory
without any access to justice, unions, or
democracy!
We're not 'accidentally' trapped in this job's
roller-coaster ride
Where fairness and compassion are repeatedly
denied
and demanding pay equity is a constant fight
But we know we must unite to demand all our
rights!
Our resistance prevails - we won't go quietly
into the night!
Resist their plans to divide; our power comes
when we unite
The change we need to see comes only with
Solidarity
There is no justice4workers without fixing the
racial divide

Each day more workers realize we are all on the
same side
This is what the scorched earth needs for us to
come out alive
The healing solution IS international socialist
revolution
If we unite to unleash our worker-led collective
might
As allies defend each other & demand policies
are right
with Solidarity power we can honor our
Indigenous treaties, transform punishment into
justice, & restore true democracy.

The Pugilist

The deafening roars
Of the crowd
Heats up my blood
Adrenaline burning
Through every cell
Muscles relaxed
Hardened springs with
Jaw-breaking power
Waiting to explode
Hands and knuckles
Covered with ass-whopping leather

I hear my name
Amidst thundering applause
"In the red corner..."
Months of training
Barrels of sweat
Beating bags, people,
Myself
All leading to this moment
A crisp and clear clarity
Shatters the cacophony

Weapons at the ready
Knees
Elbows
Fists
Feet

Brain
Muscles
Working together
A violent ballet
Synchronized and
Chaotic

Together we plunge
Into the depths of human despair
And soar to
Heights of the unconquerable
A battle of minds among
Equals
Warfare of wits among
Warriors
Belligerent intelligence
Biting into our pain
Yielding to gain

Let's Talk Racism

It Hurt

By Lincoln Alexander Estridge

The summer of 2020 hurt me
I know for a fact it hurt Many
I was afraid to drive around my neighbourhood
Afraid to encounter ex-slave catchers in my
neighborhood
The legacy of colonialism runs deep
6. Feet.
We watched Innocent Black & Brown bodies
drop like flies
As time flew, At the hands and knees of these
officers
These officers who felt entitled to bodies
As colonizers felt they were to land and bodies
of water
not too long ago.
Not too long ago,
These officers were organized to catch and kill
people that look like me
The Summer of 2020,
I was wondering if they'd ever Take A Day OFF.
Wondering if my mom will ever get tired of
Reminding me to "take my hood off in stores".
Even when it's cold because 'they' don't need a
reason

And you might look like who 'they're' looking
for.
All because the system isn't broken.
The system works fine.
The Summer of 2020 showed us that.
It Hurt. Still does.
Birthed from Colonialism and
Nursed on prejudiced and Hate for over 400+
Years
To grow into this.
I hate this.
Destructive This.
Upsetting and Hurtful This.
This is Disgusting.
I can be honest.
I was scared of This.
I was scared
when the police followed my siblings
Home from Youth Service
I was scared when the police knocked on my
door
Because I looked like Me
And that I looked like someone I wasn't.
Obviously, there are so many with worse stories
But I won't lie and Say it didn't hurt
Because TRUTHFULLY
It did.
Hurt.

Divided

"You're going to the White Man land, so better be wary
Obey the White man's law my son, don't be an adversary
Be on your best behaviour be safe while we're apart!"
These were my father's words to me as I prepared to depart

This statement wasn't racist, but pragmatic to its core
I shook my head and mumbled, "absolutely dad, for sure"
The warning has stayed with me now decades after the fact
It is the voice inside my head, guiding my every act

People in the country I was from were divided, brown and black
A gift the British colonizers used as a diversionary attack
Easier to rule by dividing and sowing seeds of hate
A tried and proven tactic, a colonial boilerplate

So African and Indian fought, for scraps from
the White man's table
While he pillaged and he plundered, they fought
over labels
Arguing about who was superior, between black
and brown skin
Like if superiority can be measured by the
amount of melanin

Now political parties use the same principles of
division
Listen carefully to what I say and heed my
admonition
None can hide from the impact of colonialism
and bondage
The journey of healing will never start until this
truth is acknowledged

Black

Black is not a colour
It is who I am
But that does not prevent me
From also being human

My lived experience is very different
From your reality
But that does not deprive me
Of my humanity

I've been orphaned from my home
Without identity
That will be my cross to bear
My internal agony

Systems designed to subdue me
Try to rob me of my pride
Yet I will fight for justice and
I will not be pacified

Forget the cause or consequence
I will not stand by
Fighting with my very last breath
I must, just to survive

Schism

When we demonize the other
Whether our enemy or our brother
In the sand, we draw battle lines
Filled with danger, laden with mines
Then there is no turning back
Chipping the armour until it cracks;
No longer fighting human beings
Just animals that deserve a beating
When we justify evil intentions
Hide them in pious inventions
Nothing they say is good or right
They are furthest from the light
We cast the roles of god and devil
One is holy, the other evil
Wrapped in moral indignation
So begins the denigration
But we are furthest from the truth
Painting our enemy as uncouth
This crutch is our justification
To write them off as an aberration
We disparage and alienate
We malign and denigrate
Freeing our conscience to violence
Influence those sitting on the fence
 This deliberate cognitive dissonance
Does nothing but serve to imprison us
It binds us to an ideology
Mixing virtue with toxicity

It's not the path to righteousness
For it only sows divisiveness
And the further apart we are divided
The more our decisions are misguided
When every act is a conspiracy
The truth soon loses clarity
Opposing sides settle in their trenches
Building walls, constructing fences
That is not the best path forward
It leads to pain and war and torture
I beg, let's learn to disagree with each other
Without resorting to wanton slaughter

The rise and fall of hate

History's dustbin is where
You belong
Among the discarded,
Destroyed and
Dismantled things
Forgotten
Useless
Unusable
That you see
Is where you should be
You drove the daggers
Of your hateful and
Wicked thoughts into
The heart and minds
Of the people
Like butter
Their hypocrisy fell away
And they too began
To inflate
Conflate
Your insipid brands of hate
With theirs

The meek was left to inherit
The earth that you
Gleefully scorched. While mercy
Wrung her hands helplessly

Pining as the
Righteous persecuted those they
Deemed sinful
Let it burn
Build the wall
Make it great
That is all

The Lady mourns the loss
Of equality and equity
The torch once used to light the way
Now incinerates immigrant caravans
Blind religion rules the day
Not mercy
Nor love
Nor kindness
Nor compassion
Fuck the widow and the poor
We don't need them coming here no more

Then a phoenix stirs among
The ashes. Downtrodden
Not trodden down
Rising brightly, ever slowly
We are all just sinners here
We cast no judgement
We lay no blame
Come experience our humanity
Escape the rising insanity
□
But brother, I can see no colour

Oh, but you should for it exists
And it persists
Forcing me to lofty actions
In a game where the rules
Convict me
Rules designed to make me lose
My only sin is
My melanin

What Was The Plan?

By Loretta Laurie Fisher

Were these Colonizers minds and hearts
removed to drum up this mayhem so deadly?
Or did they simply bend their religion into deep
racial hostility
Was it superiority, or was it undiagnosed
insanity?
Equating european complexions with the color
of god and angels and so-called normal
humanity
Re-branding all African complexions to equate
with evil, to be seen & heard as profanity
Darker skin still often deemed as if the most
undesirable; mis-labeled inferior and marked for
exclusion
Dismissed rudely without any thought of
restitution
because 'not seeing racism' sounds like a handy
solution!
The plan was always to put us aside
The plan was always to divide
The plan was always genocide.
The plan was they could always hide
Safely behind the word civilized.

Hate

What drives you to hate another
Be them friend or foe or brother
How is it you sleep at night
How do you justify that right?

Just because I say I am offended
Because my life has been upended
You rain down insults on my name
Someone who has just been shamed?

When we do this to each other
Why then do we even bother
All we do is sow more hate
When all we say infuriates

You hate me because I'm not like you
Coloured, gay, oh, and lesbians too
You say God told you to act this way
Or he'd bring about your doomsday

But hate is not what your God teaches
Love and Forgiveness is what He preaches
So, tell me again what drives your hate?
Which god gives you your mandate?
□
Love your neighbour as you love yourself
When did that get put on the shelf?
You're to love me through thin and thick

It's the Holy Spirit that convicts

It's so much easier to dehumanize
Useless animals can be euthanized.
But that house is built on shifting sand
And is destroyed by your God's own hand

You do not need an excuse
There is no need for you to choose
Your hate serves a purpose
Because it's good for business

Still Not Free

By Loretta Laurie Fisher

What's the problem? We are still in apartheid for
starters.
Why are Black people still not free to cross
borders?
We're wrongly assumed to be 'on the run', or 'on
the loose'
So many of us systematically automatically
accused
Of absolutely nothing, simply seeking refuge
but the response is to get so callously refused
So many families broken apart under this legal
ruse
So many individuals caged like animals &
subject to abuse!
Imagine this done to you – there's no way to get
out of it!
The mind-boggling, people-hogging injustice of
it!
Authorities claim to despise dreaded human
trafficking, yet
they deploy callous spies and colder people you
couldn't get
to be sneaky lookouts for neighbors they call
sneaky!
People they believe 'do not deserve' to be happy,

or to be 'real' citizens even when we 'apply' to
be
The intent is we're meant to be denied and
called 'wannabe'
Simply because we chose this place to bring our
family
We get harassed as the class they cast as the
lowest
Is it european, caucasian? No, it's African north
or west
Instead of helpful lawyers, for years get a legal
barbed-wire fence
Held in detention centres where tears don't
penetrate the cement
When we asked for 'asylum' here, this is NOT
what we meant!

Black Lives Matter

I search for peace among the pieces of my
broken life
All I find is the empty hope of a better afterlife
Dignity stolen, I stand broken, bereft of belief
Loved ones sing a lonely hymn, stricken in their
grief

History and ancestry purloined, as I am led to
market
Once a treasure, my black skin, has now become
a target
Whipped and beaten, dragging chains pining for
the past
Eyes that beheld Africa's beauty, now remain
downcast

Brutality and cruelty imprinted on my psyche
But I still hold on to the hope that one day I'd be
free
Chains and whips hurt bone and skin, but I will
not be broken
In my mind, I'm proud and free, not some
slaver's token

You institutionalize slavery and call it
segregation
All you did was repackage it and move it from
the plantation

I've got to know my place in line, or end up
hanging from a tree
This might not be called slavery, but I'm still
sure as hell not free
□

Malcolm X, Rosa Parks and Martin Luther King
Junior
Fighting for our right to freedom, fighting for
our future
One by one they strike them down, beaten to the
ground
We all will continue to take up the fight, our
message won't be drowned

A hundred years have come and gone the
struggle remains
They tell me that I've been set free, but I stand
here still in chains
Through decades of torture suffering and pain,
we stand here torn and tattered
But we will fight to our last breath because our
Black Lives - they Matter

We Are Not Intruders

By Loretta Laurie Fisher

We dream about Canada believing it's a great country to love
bringing our best qualifications, but then we're pre-judged
Seen immediately as 'illegal' people who aren't flesh & blood
Meanwhile so many people from other parts of the world
are accorded the rights and respect everyone deserves
their cultures don't get prodded into inhumane herds
by Immigration liars who don't give any reason or rhyme
while BIPOC walking freely gets twisted into high crime
deemed horribly fraudulent by lies we hear on prime-time.

215 - A poem of solidarity

Two hundred and fifteen lives
    Ripped from our tribe's embrace
Two hundred and fifteen children
    Killed by heartless holiness
We are two hundred and fifteen
    But how many more of us has there been?
In the name of a father
We never wanted
At the will of a ruler
We never belonged to
Robbed of our Tribe
    And our Family
Tried to erase our Language
    And our Spirituality
Stole our Culture
    And our Identity
In the name of a father
We never needed
At the will of a ruler
Who was not ours?
Forced whiteness
    Upon our beautiful skin
Imposed religion
    To change us from within
Talking about a god of love
    While beating us to get rid of our 'sin'
In the name of a father

We were taught to fear
At the will of a ruler
Who did not care?
This was no school
       This soulless prison
This was about torment
       Never tuition
Designed to destroy
       For the sake of religion
In the name of a father
We do not believe in
Who wants to save us
Through his immoral sin

In closing

I sought a fitting way to conclude
Our transcendental journey
Though not oft filled with rectitude
And often unquestionably wordy

I thought to end on a good note
To you my dearest reader
A silly line, a funny quote
But I could think of neither

So instead, I wish you well
As you go about your life
I pray that my words were able to dispel
Some of your struggle and your strife

Thank you to my fellow poets
Who gave their talent to this book
I am sure you already know it,
I respect your handiwork

May your words strike at the readers heart
May they serve as admonition
I pray your words will play their part
To better understand the human condition.

Poets Bio

Brian Sankarsingh is a Trinidadian-born Canadian immigrant who describes himself as an accidental poet, with a passion for advocacy and a penchant for prose. Arriving in Canada in the 1980s, Brian worked tirelessly to forge a life and career for himself. In so doing, he inadvertently shrouded his love for poetry. Now, with his children all grown up, he has rediscovered his voice.

With renewed vigour and an unapologetic style, Sankarsingh is committed to maddeningly screaming his poetic ponderings from whatever rooftop or soapbox he can find. Wading into controversial topics like systemic racism and politics, Sankarsingh's readers should think about his poetry as social and political commentary.

J.L. Kaytor has been writing since she was a teen, but credits Brian Sankarsingh, for encouraging her to take her writing to the next level.

J.E. Rehel does not consider themselves a poet but loves to play the instrument (usually in private) nonetheless. They work daily as a writer in pursuit of truth and in service of justice and beauty in Toronto.

My original name is Loretta. I've reclaimed it with my rights. As the author of poetry published in various anthologies, I'm also an Elder in Toronto's Partnership & Accountability Circle, with an opportunity to advise City Council. In the spirit of both African and Indigenous traditions I'm ready to embrace the role into the future.

Sherman K. Francis has only recently started documenting his poetry and utilizing his gift as a poet. His main aim is to allow the written word to awaken in those who read an appreciation for live and love.

Jayson-Tyler Sankarsingh has written poems recreationally from young age to creatively discuss both personal and social issues.

Lincoln Alexander Estridge is a Christian self-motivated entrepreneur, who seeks to inspire and improve his and the lives around him by being an example of what God can do and being the role model, he needed, when he was younger.

www.ingramcontent.com/pod-product-compliance
Lightning Source LLC
Chambersburg PA
CBHW011929050726
47591CB00009B/2398